Dear Hattie,

Thank you for purchasing my book. I hope the reading will be inspirational and spiritually accepted.

I am happy to know that you married Darrel, my cousin and you are rooted in the family both ways.

May God Bless You enrichly in your business. Thank You!

Love,
Julia M. Hayes

Julia M. Hayes: A Teacher's Journal

"Dare to Believe that Religion plays a Major Role in Disciplining Your Children"

By

Julia M. Hayes

authorHOUSE™

1663 LIBERTY DRIVE, SUITE 200
BLOOMINGTON, INDIANA 47403
(800) 839-8640
WWW.AUTHORHOUSE.COM

First published by AuthorHouse 12/09/04

ISBN: 1-4184-2538-9 (e)
ISBN: 1-4184-2537-0 (sc)

Library of Congress Control Number: 2004096095

Printed in the United States of America
Bloomington, Indiana

This book is printed on acid-free paper.

Dedication

to my mother, tommie I. glover

my daughters, tannish and angelia

my grandchildren, james and jasmine

The Purpose of this Book

The purpose of this personal journal is to discuss education and how Christian values can play a major role in helping to discipline a child who has "Bad Behavior" at home, in school, and in society.

After teaching in the public schools for many years, I realized how a child's conduct could affect his inability to learn effectively. And for a child to succeed academically, he must strive to keep a good attitude and personality because they are just as important as his ability.

Most of my life has been geared to education and religion. Therefore the context of this book will reflect upon an accurate and explicit account of real life's occurrences in education without biases, and my perspective on religion which is based on my Christian Faith. I also will recapitulate glimpses of my early childhood rearing, my family values, and the path in which I took to get educated and planted seeds in children lives. Finally, it will provide questions for you to consider. How would you answer them? Think about it! And what would you say about the question, "What is Bad Behavior to you?" How would you define its meaning?

My answer is simple. That is, I believe that Bad Behavior refers to the qualities of a child's actions that are below standards or below par. It also refers to attitudes that are considered morally wrong, naughty, displeasing, and unpleasant habits which might cause injury to ones self and others in every day life.

However, I know that there is no real road map to follow to increase goodness in a person to change his bad behavior, but there are certain characteristics that a person may inherit from his parents and societal influences that could affect him in the way that he acts; and possible could improve his radical behavior.

Listed Below are Several Characteristics that Reflect "Bad Behavior" from my point of view.

- ❖ Child is destructive

- ❖ Child is rude and disrespectful to others

- ❖ Child is always on the defensive side

- ❖ Child makes sarcastic remarks to hurt others feeling

- ❖ Child is disobedient to parents and teachers

- ❖ Child is slothful

- ❖ Child is selfish – concerned only with himself

- ❖ Child creates disturbances

- ❖ Child uses profanity, slang, or derogatory terms

- ❖ Child steals

- ❖ Child is abusive, insulting, and belligerent to others

- ❖ Child threatens others

- ❖ Child smokes

- ❖ Child maybe a drug abuser

- ❖ Child verbally abuses others

- ❖ Child is always on the offensive side

- ❖ Child is ill-tempered

The Author Speaks

Can you imagine growing up in rural Henry County, McDonough, Georgia, where dreams were the center of ones life? Only those who are dreamers can understand what I mean. As a child, I use to find the highest limb that I could reach in a big tree to sit on to dream of my future. *I was Tom boyish.* I could climb trees as well as my brothers could. Eventually I realized sitting in a tree was not the place for a girl to be. So I decided to take my dreams somewhere else. I began to keep them in my mind. I dreamed of being someone special in the world some day; one who would make a difference in society, one who would help others to make their lives better, and one who cared about human nature and mankind.

My dreams included that one day I would become a lucrative business woman, sitting in a big plush office, leather back chairs, designer's telephones with several employees working under me as their manager and owner of the business. But in that area, my dreams became a myth. They never came true. I worked in a business for a few years, but that was not the dream.

I came from a large family, the fourth child of fourteen children; three of them deceased, and eight of them were at home always during my childhood.

It was very difficult for me to use my imagination and dreams because there were so many chores to do. Therefore I knew I had to turn my dreams into reality. As I looked back over my childhood, I realized how closely related to poverty level we were, which meant one could only hope and dream of growing out of poverty before it set in.

Briefly I will reflect upon some of the memories of my childhood and how they have affected me today.

The only role models we had were our parents, teachers, and religious leaders. During that time, I did not realize how important they were to me because I was looking for the nameless.

My father was a brick mason, who did extremely good work. Some of his work still stands today. He was called into the ministry of the Gospel at an early age and became a Baptist preacher. My mother was a housewife because it was too many of us to hire a baby sitter for her to do public work. My mother was a Baptist too until she joined the Pentecostal Church of God and Christ. One thing I did learn early on was we may have been poor in wealth or things, but we were rich in the Love of God.

My parents were faith builders, and very resourceful. They would often talk to us about believing in what we were doing. They would tell us to believe in ourselves. They wanted all of us to get a good education, and they reminded us that without it, we would not be able to grow above poverty level in this society. And they were right!

They made sure that we had plenty of food by planting large vegetable gardens. I could hardly wait until the Fall of the year came. It was harvest time! We had all kinds of vegetables, watermelons, cantaloupes, strawberries, muscadines, berries, pecans, and other fruits. They also raised pigs and chickens. Therefore we had plenty of meat. We were never hungry.

In my early years in school, I distinctly remember grades sixth, seventh, and eighth. Those were my most crucial years. I barely had changing clothes. My sisters and I had to share everything. We wore hand-me-down clothes almost every year in school. I decided that I would not let that bother me. I was going to focus in on being an "A" student in view of the consequences. I was not always an "A" student, but I made it a point to let my teachers and parents know how interesting I was in getting my lesson every day and doing well in school. I was able to help my siblings with their schoolwork too. My father always bragged on me. He predicted the future for me. He always said I would be the "teacher in the house." I was not aware that I would become a teacher at that time, but I did my best because I did not want to let my family down and I wanted to represent them well. Also, I did not know what my father meant about "school teacher". I knew that I must have shown some kind of interest in education, but my goals were capturing the business world. I had to set goals to meet the challenges of tomorrow, I thought. However, teaching was not a part of my plan.

As I can recall, the best role model other than my mother was my 4-H Club Teacher. In my eyes, she was the greatest and most perfect person in the world. She had such wonderful characteristics. I decided that when I grew up, I would be just like her. She was witty and gave all of her student's respect. She did not mind touching us or giving us a hug. She was beautiful, and well dressed at all times. And she taught us so many things about real life situations. She developed good building blocks and social skills for us. She taught us how to be respectful to everyone. And on certain occasions, she suggested to us how to make use of what we had. She had a good sense of humor and often quoted the old cliché that "the opportunity does not come by but once, take advantage of it while it is there." I was not sure then of what she was saying, but later on in life, I realized exactly what she was trying to convey to us. Many times she would say to us if you are going to be a winner, be the best winner, speak correct English, do not be distracted easily by nonsense matters, stay focused, and always have a good sense of humor. Mrs. Jones inspired me to set goals for the future and adhere to them. Even today, I am a retired teacher who is still reaching out to help others who need me because I know how important it is to remove myself and show that I genuinely care for others. As I approached my junior year in high school, I was faced with the "impossible Dilemma." What would I now do? What would I become! Just what would I do to become the person whom I was seeking? At that time, I had no directions. All I knew was that I enjoyed reading about the natural environment, reading the Bible, the newspaper, comic books, novels, short stories, plays, completing crosswords puzzles in the newspaper, observing small creatures in nature such as: bees, ants, spiders, butterflies, wasps, June bugs fireflies, birds, and worms. They caught my eye because they were so beautiful. Also at night, I would sit out and observe the moon as it moved across the sky and wondered about the dark areas in it. The older people would tell us that those dark areas were the "Devil beating his wife with a stick." Of course I did not believe that. Later in life, I learned that those dark areas were related to volcanoes, hot lava flow, and craters interaction on the moon. As the sun arose in the morning I began to wonder what was causing it to move across the sky. What was holding it up there? I had heard my teachers talk about gravity, but I did not grasp the real understanding of its functioning because I could not see it. Then I thought, the sun is one of God's Heavenly bodies and only He could control its movement. I learned that there were so many things about God that we did not understand. I had to study to show myself approved. Today scientists call the sun one of the Celestial bodies. Little did I know that science was going to be one of my favorite subjects to teach for many years. I really did not like teaching science at first, because math was my favorite subject. It did not matter that I had a hard time understanding math in my middle grades. As time went by, I began to study more and it became very clear to me in my Junior and senior years in school. When I began to teach, I taught math more than any other subject throughout my teaching career.

After graduating from high school the real test came. I did not forget my home training. God was always first in our house. And serving Him was a major part of our daily lives. We had to attend Sunday school, and church and take part in the worship service. I was trained to be a Junior Sunday school Teacher and taught classes for a few years.

That is when I realized my teaching ability. But I had no idea that it would lead to 32 years of teaching experiences. I participated in the church programs and helped with planning them. I sang in the youth choir and the adult choir for years.

Then it was time for college. I was the first one to go to college and graduated in my family. I had several plans in mind, but Business College was my first choice. I was not sure that I was making the right decision, but as usual, I prayed over it and began my studies. I spent a few years going to Business College and graduated, but was not successful in finding the right job. The struggle of finding the right job in the 60's was very disappointing. There was no place for black women in the business world. My credentials became null and void. The only job that I could find was typing, taking little dictation in shorthand, or telephone solicitation. Those jobs did not pay much. One could not afford to live off of that salary. You could work in a cafeteria or restaurant and make more money.

However, many black women took those jobs and stayed with them for the sake of status. I tried it, but it did not work for me. Eventually I quit and went into something else. After working in several capacities, I decided it was time for me to get a real job. I began to challenge myself. One day I went to the City Hall downtown Atlanta. I ran across an article that read, "Career Opportunity Program, a work study program." Immediately I thought this must be something that I needed to look into. I read the job description, which stated, "Do you want more education? More money, etc.? I said to myself, YES! I want more money and better working conditions. This must be for me! I thought. I began to Thank God! I filled out all necessary paperwork, took the test, and passed. Now I was headed into a new career – EDUCATION!

Table of Contents

Destined to be a Teacher

Somehow I knew this was for me because I truly believe that God had my name on it. Also, this is the time when I regarded my father's words, "she will be the teacher in the house."

That was the first time I thought that teaching must be my destiny. However, I began to wonder what would I be in this program if I were accepted. Will I be a teacher? Well, I was accepted and the program solved that for me. It was geared to teachers only. This time I had no doubt.

Again I reflected back to my father's words, "She will be the teacher in the house." I wondered how did he know. But because of his faith I was ready to meet the challenge. My character became an important aspect then. I had to show it in everything that I was doing especially in education.

I vividly remembered the words of Dr. Martin Luther King, Jr. When he spoke of a man's character and education. He said, "the Black and the poor should rise up from poverty level to a more meaningful or moral level." At that time, I needed some help with this passage because I was not sure if I was on poverty level or not and did I have my morals in the right place? When I was growing up, it seemed that everybody in my neighborhood was living under the same condition, and it was okay with me. And I did not know much about low-socio-economic level, whether it was high or low when it came to finances. After giving this passage considerable thought, I believe that he was referring to a man's character as being all of the qualities or features that are typical to distinguish him from other persons, groups, or things such as: individual nature, moral values, moral qualities, moral strength, integrity, capacity to learn academically, economic level, attitude, status, disposition, or behavior." Therefore, I knew that I had many of those qualities, but I must put them into action. I also needed the guided force of nature to lead me. That is when I really began to have faith in what I was doing.

Helen Steiner Rice once wrote..."but nothing in life that is worthy – Is ever too hard to achieve – If you have the faith to believe... For faith is a force that is greater than knowledge or power or skill – and many defeats turn into triumph – if you trust in God's wisdom and will."

After reading this poem, from that moment on, I began to trust God for all of my needs more than ever. I was a little reluctant to go to Georgia State University because of my experiences with them in the past. But I chose it any way as my college to further my education. It was more than just a thought. I had not realized how much prejudice tension was out there. In fact, I was sheltered at home and my parents did not talk about segregation or integration to us. Therefore I did not know very much about discrimination, especially against black Americans until I got to GSU. My goal was to keep in mind that the reality of racial prejudice did exist. But it would not interfere with my objectives to earn the degrees I was seeking.

As I worked daily, I kept relying on what my teacher said in high school about staying focused. I had a goal in mind and I was going to pursue it. At that time, the consequences did not matter. A few years back, I tried to enroll into GSU when I first came out of high school and I remember the number of times they refused to let me in. Finally I gave up and went to Dimery's Business College, graduated, and did not think of GSU any more until this opportunity came along. I was accepted in GSU without any problem, now that my finances were a guarantee and my tuition was paid.

Well the journey began. GSU was a challenge for me. Most of the time, I was the only Black American in class. Many times, the instructor expressed that a few of us would not be able to master nor understand the skills being taught. We were given the option to drop the classes while we had the opportunity to get a refund back. Those words made me that much more determined to meet the professors head-on. I would show them that I could follow instructions and understood the

lesson. I did not give up. I mastered all skills required to receive a Bachelor's Degree in Elementary Education in three and a half years and graduated. I made the Dean's list at least four times. I was BLESSED. I was hired immediately as a teacher. What an experience! The country was in the middle of a Segregation-Integration crisis. But I knew that I could not let it hinder me. I had to stay focused.

As I taught from day to day, I realized something was missing. I kept reflecting upon what Dr. Martin Luther King, Jr. fought so hard for. He wanted us to become educated to the highest level of our potential that was achievable.

Dr. Martin Luther King, Jr.

I had a lot of faith in Dr. King and his work because he was the leader of the black community during those years. Therefore I went back to graduate school and earned a Master's Degree in Education for Middle Grades, and a M.ED Degree in Data Collecting, from GSU. Later, I took a course of study at Emory University in **CULTURES**: **(The Center for Urban Learning/Teaching and Urban Research in Education and Schools**). With those degrees, I was able to master the kind of classroom teaching that I felt the students needed to have to become great achievers. Those degrees played a major role in my teaching and in knowing how to deal with students on almost every level and I saw mastery work from many of them as well.

Teaching at school was not just enough for me to help meet the needs of children who had a hard time in academics. Later on, I helped to develop a Tutorial Program where I became an Administrator to help build a connection between homework and schoolwork, which lasted for about five years. Not only did I tutor young children, but high school, college level and adults in many other fields as well. I knew that education carried a certain amount of status with it, which meant I had to possess professional qualities, exemplifying a well-rounded person with good citizenship, good moral values at all times, and build a good foundation for the students whom I was teaching.

I started with myself by building a stronger relationship with God. I pressed to have more faith in my students, colleagues, family, church and my community. Each day, I put God at the head of my life. I developed my own ideas as to how I would interact with the students. Since prayer was an integral part of my daily life, then secondly, I must be patience and wait on an answer from God after praying, thirdly, I must be persistent with my prayers and finally, I had to persevere or continue to press for the right things to happen each day.

As I began to work my plan, the **4- "Ps", I call them, (Prayer, patience, persistence, and perseverance)**, I began to see improvement in my teaching. I decided that no matter what happened I would always love and trust God, and humanity regardless of their personalities and attitudes.

My parents taught me how to be obedient to them, and kept me in God centered places where examples of living a Christian life were prevalent. I had to learn how to be obedient to God myself.

My goal was to create an environment that would reach every child whom I was teaching by introducing life's skills that would help shape and mold them and assist with their future.

Over the years, I taught students how to be obedient through a variety of ways. I started out with simple skills that required simple directions and logical thinking. Since I was the role model for them, I had to be realistic, honest, humble, and dependable. I taught them that social ties were very important in the home, the school, the church, and in society. They had to learn the importance of moral values as well. I often asked the students questions that would create a stimulus for thinking, such as: How strong are your social values in your home? Your school? and your church? Very few of them could express or explain what was happening in any of those places because they could not understand the word "strong." Once I explained how the word "strong" related to their environment, they were able to answer the question. I used questions such as" when you encounter a crisis especially if you are home alone, who would you contact for help? What would you do? Then I was able to get a reasonable answer.

Many days I would be called upon to fill the shoes of a doctor, a nurse, a mom, a dad, a friend, a coach, a money changer, a safe keeper, a politician, a taxi driver, a psychologist, a cook, a faith builder, and a shoulder to cry on. Those days were fine for me, because I wanted to make sure that I was the central focus in the students' lives while they were in school. I wanted them to learn how to take in knowledge and how to impart it.

After reading Marva Collins' book, I noticed that she had gone through some of the same difficult situations as I had. And after listening to her lecture once, I knew that she worked well with the 4-"Ps" too. (Prayer, patience, persistence, and perseverance) I could hear it in her voice. She mentioned in her book that she had to be "a warrior in battle, doing battle against peer pressure, fear, prejudice, negativity, disrespect, -- but fought back with grace, love, obedience, faith, kindness, laughter, and the whole Armor of God." She also stated that "children respected teachers who at all times showed that they were concerned about their welfare."

I agreed with Marva Collins because she was so opened and honest with her feeling about teaching students. As I taught over the years, I managed to get through the day with" the **4- P's**, faith, showing respect, love, commitment and a good sense of humor with my students because I knew that they wanted to be treated fairly. And I would not teach in any other way.

I am a product of the Civil Rights Movement; when Dr. Martin Luther King, Jr., Mayor Maynard Jackson, Dr. Ralph D. Abernathy, Rev. Jessie Jackson, Ambassador Andy Young, Dr. Benjamin E. Mays, and Congressmen John Lewis were in power as politicians, educators, and great leaders who worked very hard to help transform our country into one America rather than two. I had great respect for those men because they were constantly engaged in programs such as Civil Rights, Equal Rights, and Justice for the betterment of all people.

I wondered why they did not stress to the law makers how important it was to keep *prayer* in the public school system. I remember when prayer was taken out of the public school. I was crushed by that decision because I could not imagine how anyone could go a day without acknowledging God. After observing Dr. Martin Luther King very closely, I noticed that he always prayed before or during his marches. And I knew that taking prayer out of the public schools was a mistake. And with this knowledge, I began to understand Dr. Martin Luther King, Jr's mission better. I thought that our country was built on God's word. I remember reciting the Lord's Prayer and or the 23rd Psalms in school for many years. As I recall, in my last three years in high school how the students' attitudes were beginning to change. I believe that their attitudes were changing because they did not have to respect the guiding force of nature between them, academics and social skills because we no longer had to recite the Lord's Prayer, the 23rd Psalm or sing religious songs any more. We had a choice.

Many students did not choose carefully and made the wrong choice. I regret that the lawmakers made that decision to take *prayer* out because someone felt that it was unconstitutional. Today "Prayer" has become "**NULL** and **VOID**." Now we see the consequences of that decision. Instead of "Prayer" in the public schools, we have the "Moment of Silence." For many students it means **NOTHING**!. Some of them are very inconsiderate of others feeling. They do not get quiet neither do they respect those who are quiet and would like to participate in this "Moment of Silence." Many students have to be reminded day after day that this is *reflection time*. They find it to be totally insignificant. In my opinion, the lawmakers, parents, nor educators expected the students to portray such awful behavior during this *reflection time*. They probably thought that it would be a smooth transition. Therefore they have become disappointed in their children. Many teachers are disappointed too. They are saying that this is really not working.

Parents' Role

I dare parents to believe that religion plays a major role in disciplining their children and steering them in the right directions. Parents should put more effort into preparing their children for school each day. This will alleviate the teacher from having to correct behavior in conduct daily and during *reflection time*. They should teach self-esteem and respect for others at home and this will give the teacher more time to teach academics in school. Parents should articulate to their children the Christian values that are important to the family structure and in society. They should instill into them that certain ethics are just plainly understood or old fashioned methods of home training is necessary for survival in this world. The parent should show criticism in a positive way; perhaps it will encourage positive attitudes and personalities among their children and hopefully they will not be so eager to judge or condemn others. Parent must always remember that they are the role models. If they are constantly fighting in front of their children, this teaches them how to be hostile. Many times parents' tolerance level is very low because they would have had a hard day; they may take it out on their children. This attitude will teach their children to be impatient. Parents' should praise their children for the good that they do, this will instill confidence and appreciation in their efforts. And parents must be fair and honest with their children, in this way they will develop a love for themselves and others.

Determined to be the BEST!

I strongly believe that because I was raised up in a Christian environment, and moral standards were a must in my home, it has made a difference in the way I act today. If I had not been taught moral values and Christian values in my home first, then academics in school secondly, I may not have understood the right course to take in life. I still confess my faith in those beliefs. I believe that without God, man has anything to fear, perhaps because he puts his confidence and faith in something or someone else. For example: *Science* or *Politics*. What do you think?

If man's confidence and all of his faith is in science and politics alone, then he has no power to interact with the universe.

Yes, we have learned so much about life through those areas, especially space exploration. Scientists have examined the earth's atmosphere, its hydrosphere, its biosphere, and down to the core of the earth thoroughly. And we are aware that because of exploration, we have learned a wealth of knowledge in academics and about God's heavenly bodies. However children of today are living in the crucial millennium Age that steer them in the direction of capitalism which eliminates the idea of religion of any kind of God as being their guiding force. Consequently, many scientists and people in general have forgotten that their knowledge of the earth's exploration was introduced and directed by God's intervention because it was not man's idea to begin with. Therefore, in as much as we have studied today, we are still learning that scientific knowledge is limited when it comes to God's creation.

After being an educator for 32 years, following the guidelines of the school system and its curriculum, I still find myself searching for new methods for teachers who are teaching with disciplining problems or children with "bad conduct" in the classroom. I felt that I was successful in my teaching, but was never satisfied with some students' natural behavior in conduct. What more could I have done to help them understand that *self-respect* and *self-discipline* are two very important concepts in learning academically? Conduct has become a problem nationwide in our public schools. What is the solution to this problem? Who has the authority or power to make this change in children's behavior? Parents? Teachers? or **God**?

I imagined walking into the classroom one day observing the students and their behavior, working busily at their own pace, completing assignments, or doing something constructive without the teacher standing before them giving instructions every moment. Physically, I wanted to see them working out of harmony, peace, and love, together without me having to pressure them to complete their assignments and show good conduct while they were actually learning to their maximum potential.

"Gone are those days" when a teacher can assign many students work and they will complete it without the teacher giving instructions over and over again, throughout the entire lesson. Reason why? Many students do not feel that they need to listen to directions. Neither do they seem to be interested in education. What is it going to take to wake them up?

In my early years of teaching I saw students with great potential and enthusiasm in their work habits. Their parents seemed to have been more concerned and supportive to the school whole heartily. They demanded respect from their children and expected them to learn academically. They would not only put pressure on their children at home to complete all homework, but checked with the teacher frequently to see it they had done all of their schoolwork as well.

10

Today it is different. Time has changed. Many parents do not have the time to spend with their children because of the burden that society has cast upon them. The parents are always trying to make it better for their children than what they had. I have heard them say that many times.

They are purchasing big houses, new cars, all the latest fashions in clothing for their children, costly summer vacations, and getting their children in every sport attainable which has put them in a financial bond of having to work two or three jobs to meet their needs. Therefore they do not have quality time with their children at home. Very rarely do you find many families sitting down eating breakfast, lunch, or dinner together. When parents are at home with their children, many of them are playing catch – up time. Seldom do they have the opportunity to watch a family program on TV. Neither do they take the time to teach their children the building blocks of becoming a good character in the world. They do not have time to impart knowledge such as: good study habits, loving God or developing a good Bible base program at home and at church. If parents expect for their children to become productive, wholesome, patient, law-abiding citizens in society, they must not just tell them how to do it, but they must demonstrate the old cliché, don't do as I say, but do as I do!

During my last ten years of teaching, I could really see a transformation in the students' behavior. I could tell immediately which child came from a home where they were taught morals and values consistently. Those students would come to class each day prepared to work. They would have their homework ready and would follow through the entire day. They were well mannered and respectful. And they always stood up for the right thing in class. However, there were those students whose parents were either working all the time, not at home for one reason or another, broken homes, either living with the mother or the father, sometimes with other relatives, or friends of the family. Many times these children would have a hard time adjusting to their living conditions. And because some of them cannot adjust well, they become aggressive to their classmate and sometimes to their teacher in a negative way.

I have had students to tell me that they had to stay at their friend's house over night because their parents were having problems. Therefore they could not do their homework because their books were at home.

Just thinking about those children and the irregularities that encountered their lives, made me feel helpless. What could I do to help them? And how could I reach them? I knew it was not my fault that the children had a problem in the home, but what could I do to help the children at school? Many of them who encountered those kind of problems developed low-self esteem.

A few of them became troublemakers. Several days I just wanted to walk into the classroom and say to them – today we are going to talk about self-discipline, love for one another, peace, faith, prayer, promises, forgiveness, and building a good relationship with each other and God. I knew I could teach some of those concepts and others I could not, perhaps because I dare not mention nor taught anything about GOD! I will never criticize education in any way. The method we used to teach academically was the best if life's situations would fit into that mold. And education has been good for me. However, sometimes I felt deprived because it was such little I could do in the classroom with expressing my feelings about doing things in a Christian way. I felt hopeless, or a lack of growth in my teaching style because I had to minimize the role of my Christian Faith based on the ethics of the Constitution of the United States of America and the public school system.

What has happened to the freedom of expression?

As I refer back to my grade school years when my teachers told us that the first book that was written for knowledge and read in school was the Bible. Why have we let it go? I guess the same reason that the Lord's Prayer was taken out of the public schools. Or is it because we live in a pluralistic society where God is used only when we see fit?

Critics' Point Of View

Critics, such as: politicians, educators, writers, professionals, authors, religious leaders, and many other experts in the world have said that the American society is built on "Pluralism" and "Capitalism." That seems to be what is happening today. In order to be more explicit with those terms, one must define the meaning of them. According to American Heritage Dictionary, "pluralism" means a condition of society in which numerous distinct ethnic, religions, or cultural groups coexist within one nation. And it defines "capitalism" as an economic system characterized by freedom of the market with increasing concentration of private and corporate ownership of production and distribution means, proportionate to increasing accumulation and reinvestment of profits." Well based on my experiences in the American society, both

definitions are usable. However, I feel that "religion" should be treated as a separate entity. We should be able to talk to children in the public schools about moral values relating to God, the "Supreme Being," just as we talk to them about the economy.

We should be able to teach children about prayer and tell them that it is necessary to pray for a good living and survival in the world. We should not have to wait until a disaster strikes such as: "9/11, 2001 – *The Terrorist Attack on America*," which was a wake-up call to express our feelings about God. That was the time God's name was used more frequently than ever, openly and constantly in America.

As we travel up and down the highways throughout the country today, you will find signs displaying such messages as: I am a prayer warrior, pray for peace in America, pray with out ceasing, pray for the United States, pray for our President, and pray for our country. Prayer has become an "epidemic." The TV Ministries, commentators, news reporters, writers, Talk Show Hosts, Radio Broadcasters, people in the malls, pastors in the pulpit, teachers in the classroom, and children are talking about "9/11 – 2001." And God is the central focus of those conversations and discussion without doubt. And no

one seems to be afraid to call God's name. What does this tell us about our society? To me, this is saying that many times we forget who our provider is. We use God to help us only when we need him. The teachers had no problem talking to the students about God after the "Terrorist Attack." Why cannot teachers encourage students to understand from an intellectual point of view the role that God plays in the Christian faith?

Today politicians and many others are saying that we need to put "prayer" back into the schools, or other biblical rituals such as: The Ten Commandments, or Psalms 23. Do they really mean it? Or are they just saying it to help them feel better about the Nation's wake-up call?

We all know how important our country is to us. We recite the "Pledge of Allegiance" to the flag daily. It ends with "*One Nation, under God, Indivisible, with Liberty and Justice for all.*" Do we really mean "Under God?" Think about it. What do you think? The United States money specifically articulates "IN GOD WE TRUST!" Do we really trust God? Something seems to be wrong here. The way things are, are not the way they suppose to be.

Darryl Baskin wrote in his theory, "American Pluralism" that "Pluralism safeguards American diversity. Our varied nationality, religious, racial economic, sectional, and ideological groups are both the pride and the protection of a government by the people. Our political system should reflect the rich diversity of our group life. Our society is pluralist, in short; should our government not be pluralist too?" In my opinion, I believe that Darryl Baskin point was well stated because he showed in his review that pluralism controls the extremists overtly by giving them a place in government which will enable them to have a voice in government.

Pluralism also eliminates "conflict and deprivation." So when the issue regarding religion being taught in the public schools arises, the government can always refer to the pluralist view on religion and shows where it is not *for or against* the "issue" or any one group because it cannot declare an official religion for the country since it is too broad. "The pluralist also points to the faults in the system as faults of the system." They view religion as being another *issue* such as Racial Discrimination, Poverty, Sex Abuse, and etc. Just as I do.

According to the United States Constitution, "The right to hold any or no religious belief is absolute. "The First Amendment and the First Freedoms" allege that, one should have the right and freedom of expressing his point of view on religion as he wishes in some public places, (not school) as long as he does not try to impose his religious beliefs off on others. I agree with many of those critics who say that the government should not have the authority to compel any censor creed to curb this freedom of speech unless it is endangering someone's life.

Also a person's religion should not interfere with other laws originated to protect the people or its country from peace, order, good health, and safety morals in society.

In the early 1960s "the Supreme Court ruled that reciting nondenominational prayers or the Lord's Prayer and reading the Bible violated the *establishment clause* it made part of the program of public school." After reading that article, I realized that the public school system was in trouble. I knew what had kept me going as a student in school and how prayer was the key to my success. Since we cannot use prayer in the public schools, many students are deprived of the use of the First Amendment of the United States' Constitution because they cannot openly express their feeling through prayer. This issue also deprives most educators because they realize how sensitive it is that they cannot pray openly at work. And when they are faced with problems or trouble arises in the schools for example; when teachers move from generalities to specifics" such as thinking of praying, they realize that they cannot pray because there is no protection under the law for them.

John B. Cobb, Jr. wrote in his thesis statement that, "Education broadly is the way children socialized into the culture and are prepared to play a constructive role within it. Culture cannot be separated from a pattern of values and a way of life. What we have called "religions" are traditions or "ways" that embody and transmit such values and cultural forms. **New** patterns of values and ways of life are often not thought of as *religions*, but they have the same functions, and I am considering them as alternative "ways." Every society must carry out these educational functions in some way. In the past two centuries, much of this task has been assigned to public schools."

Also Cobb, said that "The Sunday Schools that in the United States influenced the establishment of public schools were intended in part to save the souls of their students who had no other religious instruction." In my opinion, the point that Cobb was making was that "public schools were pressed to recognize cultural pluralism and to avoid favoring any one religious tradition over others. In other words, cultural neutrality is an impossible goal for public schools. However, I feel that it can be done. Teachers should be able to teach in a way so that students will be able to appreciate and understand cultural and religious differences by using "Supreme Being" terms such as: God and Jesus Christ. If children can think "UNIVERSE," they can think of who created it.

Survey I

In the year of 2003, I was asked to participate in a questionnaire called CHRISTIAN CIVIC AND POLITICAL NATIONAL RESEARCH SURVEY. This survey polled Christians who held leadership positions in the local community and were involved in Christian activities. The purpose of this survey was to show American's political leaders that Christians are becoming more politically engaged. Therefore, politicians cannot continue to ignore the concerns of Christians' wishes. There were thirty questions labeled A through F each. These questions dealt with the TRADITIONAL VALUES COALITION programs. I felt good about completing this survey because it had questions relating to the same issue that I have about religion or Christianity being taught in the public schools. I supported many questions, but the ones that I felt had an impact on my life and children of today's society were: 1) "TVC (Traditional Values Coalition) is right. The Christian faith and moral beliefs of America's founders are a key reason for why America became a great nation. Rejection of God and traditional moral norms pose a great danger to our nation and our young people. America needs strong moral leadership." 2) "The ACLUS's (Anti-Christian Left's ... assault on Christianity over the last 40 years has confused young people and weaken morality in America..." 3) "TVC has just as much right to organize Christians to have a voice in government "as the other organizations such as the Labor Unions and Liberal groups. I supported the idea of continuing to produce and distribute the highest quality books and video documentaries to children and schools on America's Christian heritage" and it should be included in our history books as references of the Christian faith and its origin in America. 4) And finally, "we should generate enormous pressure on Congress to pass the VOLUNTARY PRAYER IN SCHOOL AMENDMENT, as it has been called by President Bush." Thanks to President George Bush!

I truly supported the four questions above because I felt that if these laws would be passed by Congress, the more chances teachers would have to strengthen and reinforce good behavior in the public schools, and parents would reinforce these good Christian values and the traditional moral values in the home.

However, many parents may not support the idea of Christian values because of their religious background. They may not be a Christian and feel that science or technology are the areas that are most important because they will motivate the children to become financially successful in society, and their children will not have a behavior problem and a reason to misbehave as long as they are engaged in those secular activities. What do you think?

Disciplining Plan

A few years ago, I was teaching my students about different types of literature. We were engaged in reading Informational Books. One book in particularly caught my attention. It was entitled, *A Book about God*. This picture book illustrated the "analogy between the concepts of God and the beauty of power and nature." I was thrilled when I read the meaning of those illustrations. One short paragraph caught my view was that, "The air is like God. Air is all around us; even though we do not see it we feel its warmth and its coolness. Without air outside us and within us we cannot live. Without God we cannot live." Those words were so powerful, they created a deep sense of reverence in my life. They expressed the power of God!

They had no denominational status! I knew that if we, as teachers could be a witness for God in that manner, like the illustration in the book, we should be able to say to a child who is having problems, have you heard about God? Do you know He is the oxygen we breathe in and out our bodies each day? The wind that blows across the land and atmosphere, and He is the air we cannot see! Well, that is the way God is to us. He is a "spirit" in our lives that we cannot see, but we can feel Him in our souls. That is how we know that He is there. Again those were the years when we could not use God's name at all. We had to talk about Him as a "Super Natural force" without a name. I was not pleased with that method of teaching. That was another example of the deprivation of teaching. In many ways, the students were deprived of concepts that they should know in life. Example: Who awaken you this morning? Most children will say, "My Mom." But is that true? Think About It! What would you say?

Four years ago, my pastor asked me to direct Summer Camp 2000, which had lead to 2003 at my church, seven weeks each year. I was excited. I knew that this was my opportunity to see how religion would work if we could use it in the public school system. My pastor, Bishop James H. Morton provides a highly structured Program for the youth. The instructors use a variety of activities that promote positive behavior at all times. He gave me the authority to direct the camp with my own discretion, as long as I remembered that I was directing it in church. I had no problem with that. It was something I wanted to experience.

I always thought of the what ifs'! I was very optimistic about the idea. We would give the children the best camp experience that they had ever encountered.

I decided to test the situation. I would use certified classroom teachers, youth workers, a nutritionist expert, assistant director, and a director. The criteria for the selection of teachers

Disciplining Strategies

were that: they must have a teaching certificate, preferably in education, had taught school for at least one year, a faith based Christian background in religion, possessed the characteristics of the 4 P's (prayer, patience, persistence, and perseverance), loved children, and could get along with the children and colleagues well.

The strategy that I would use was to integrate the academics with religion and social skills.

This would be a "Religious Based Camp." We would start our day with a "Moment of Spiritual Expression to help transfrom their minds." This would include a prayer and a blessing. The camp provided breakfast, lunch and an evening snack for the campers. After breakfast, we would have our daily Inspiration, which included two praise songs or secular songs – free of derogatory terms, prayer, and a scripture. (The student campers would be in charge).

Our core subjects: Reading, Math, Science, English/Spelling, and some Computer classes would be taught in the morning. Lunch would proceed core subjects. The highlight of our day was: At 1:30 PM daily, we would drop everything and teach *Christian Education* for one hour. During this task, we would teach good Christian Characteristics by using such building blocks as: Love, Faith, Wisdom, Knowledge, Obedience, Trust, Mercy, Grace, and many other Godly characteristics through a series of Biblical stories, passages, songs, story hour, poems, Arts and Crafts, Spanish, Music and Computer Games.

Surprisingly, the student campers and the teachers were delighted. Perhaps because the teachers knew that the four "Ps" were working (prayer, patience, persistence and perseverance). The parents were elated. I never knew that this program would have such an impact on the campers, the parents, the church, the school, and the community across the country. Campers from various places around the globe attended our camp each year. People are reminding me constantly that we should have an extension to this program. When it came to conduct, we had no problem because the campers were having so much fun learning in this manner until they had no time for problems. The teachers also taught the campers how to solve their problems in a Christian way. Instead of punishment, we had a certified counselor on staff and she would counsel the campers if they became disobedient. However, this was not often because the teachers consistently reminded the campers that God loved them and they should love him. No camper was forced to adhere to these rules, they just fell in place. Each year, many of the campers would return and the same teachers would return to teach at the camp if space was available. In this way, we could track the growth in conduct and social settings of campers over the years. From the very beginning the campers and parents were told that this would be a Christian Camp and all of our activities and academics would be centered around Christian Education. The teachers looked for many ways to enhance Christian activities into their curriculum by using Bible characters or Bible stories as a framework for their lesson plans. These kinds of lessons taught the campers that Christians misbehave and do not always follow directions either. And there were consequences for them when they were disobedient too.

The children of Israel were one good example. They were lead out of Egypt by Moses. And as soon as they were free, they began to turn back to their wicked ways of disobeying God because they did not have the faith or the patience to wait on God's deliverance. Therefore God reprimanded them for not obeying His commands. Another example was a story from *The Children's Bible*, which tells the story of Saul, the first King of Israel. It tells how Samuel calls the people together to let them know how they had disobeyed God again.

And the only way they could get a King as they had asked for was to get back in good grace with God by obeying His Commandments.

The people agreed to trust God and follow His commands. Samuel presented Saul to the Israelites. Then he told the people that God had sent Saul to be their King and there was none like him. But they "must walk in the ways of the Lord and serve Him." And both, the King and they would do well. "If they went against the Commandments of the Lord, or do evil in the sight of the Lord, then the Lord's anger would be against them." These Israelites had disobeyed God before and He gave them another chance. This kind of story would introduce the campers to new knowledge, and appreciation of scriptures in the Bible that taught lessons on being obedient to God, their parents and teachers when they were away from home. This was one of our methods of teaching good conduct. We encouraged or instilled in the campers that God was always at work and we were trying to build a good relationship with Him. And since each camper was a part of the camp we expected them to follow the rules by behaving well. We had very few disruptions during the entire seven weeks each year. However, whenever a camper misbehaved, we allowed them to explain why they acted in that manner. Then we decided if prayer was needed. If so, the camper would pray for himself. This prayer would help the camper to remember not to act in that manner again. Just by using that simple method, our camp became the best, most orderly camp around. We could take our campers any place and they were well

My Belief

behaved. The last four years have shown me that we can discipline our children better in the public schools if we could use some of the methods listed above. I really have seen results using those methods. I saw children becoming independent learners, and learn how to work together in small to large groups without problems. The teachers did not have to stand over them all day long to get them to complete their assignments.

If the teachers had the opportunity to use similar methods, just think what a great day they all would have and how much learning would take place in the schools.

According to history, America was built on the foundation of ethics, vision, morals, and basic principles such as: commitment, dedication, motivation, initiative, and caring about each other. This foundation should start at home. Parents are responsible for their children and the way that they act. Parents are the authority figure in their homes and of their children lives until they become adults. "They are ultimately responsible" for their growth and development. I believe that parents should pray for their children daily so that they will do the right thing at home, at school, at church, and away from home in other places. Parents should let their children know that God is a strong figure in their lives and they should serve Him. They should explain to them the power of prayer and the value that it serves in their every day lives and in the future. Parents should be the lighthouses in their children lives. Therefore they should let their light shine so that their children can see it. I believe that parents should set goals for their children by exposing them to certain Christian values. God should be at the head of their goals. The Bible should be the motivational factor in the Christian home so that the child will act in a Godly manner always. Parents should study the Bible with their children just as they do their schoolwork. The Bible tells us "To show yourself approved."

Since society help shape and mold children into becoming mature adults in the world, they should conduct themselves in the way in which they would like to see their children act as a child and as an adult. When children leave home in the morning for school, the parents should set good ground rules for them to follow all day because their rules determine how the child will

Parents Set Goals

behave in class all day. Parents need to remind their children that education is a major part of their future, and with God in their lives they will work better in school to make better grades, get alone with their peers, develop good social habits, refrain from corruptible and disruptive behavior if they trust Him. And if they let God be in control of their lives at all times, they will see and feel the results of being a better student.

We all have preconceived notions about our children as they enter school. We think that they are the best! Therefore, when they do the wrong thing we are disappointed in them. Our President says, "Every child can Learn and no child should be left behind." The Government says that "we have over 23 million illiterates in the American's society today." Some politicians call our nation, "A Nation at Risk." And unsympathetic Press quotes "We must get morality back into the classroom." As many Americans know, America's expectation is very high and unlimited with education. Yes, we hear what all of these critics are saying about education, but what are they doing about *bad behavior in the classroom*? What are they doing to help the teachers with conduct problem?

Julia M. Hayes

Television Promotes "Bad Behavior"

Today our society promotes "Bad Behavior" by way of television. Some of the movies that are on are damaging to our children's mind. It shows a child how to become a criminal, thief, killer, or anything else that he chooses to be in the secular world. In my opinion, there are not enough religious programs on television to counteract the bad ones. When our children look at television, they hear all kinds of bad language, and see all kinds of indecent acts that portray "Bad Behavior." Parents, where are you in this? Are you monitoring the programs that your children are watching?

Life has not always been perfect or good for famous people and images can be deceiving. Most famous people look as if they do not have a problem in the world. That is the reason why our children want to emulate them. But if we listen and look at Talk Show Hosts, ET, read books about them, and watch professional shows, such as CNN News; we will learn that many famous people have had or is having their share of trials and tribulations too. However, they cannot let their guards down – they have to keep the image visible as an entertainer. And also they must play those roles to make money.

Changing A Generation

In order for our children to overcome some of the problems they are facing in the schools today, that they must learn how to speak out on the "issue" of "Bad Behavior." They must form the habit of saying to a child who is misbehaving or acting up, "You are disturbing me! Please be quiet! You are taking away my privilege to learn! I value my education! If other students in the classroom told more students that, perhaps it will dawn on them that they are crunching someone's style while they are trying to learn.

Bishop Paul S. Morton, Presiding Bishop of the Full Gospel Baptist Church Fellowship International Conference, goal is to "Change A Generation" by the "Sword of the Spirit." I admire him for his determination and dedication. He has done extensive work and research for the last ten years on how to change a person's way of thinking; especially the younger generation.

Discipline is one of Bishop Paul Morton's greatest characteristics. He speaks of people being disciplined at all time. The results of his self-discipline is seen in all of the works in his ministry. "He feels that God's people need to be orderly, on time, and well prepared even if they do not feel like it."

For those who know Bishop Paul S. Morton, can say that he exemplifies a person who is ultimately disciplined.

Well, I feel the same way that Bishop Paul S. Morton does. I believe that *education* and *religion* are two of the most important aspects of life. Many Innovated teachers and educators need to change their style of teaching and put the pressure on the parents to fulfill their duties and responsibilities at home. *Religion* and *education* are both life *skills*. If our children can read, write, think, compute math, socialize and interact with their peers, they can train themselves to obey in the right manner.

Most school systems implement a strong discipline policy on conduct, but there is still a weakness in "bad Behavior." The most drastic thing I see happening today is that we are raising up a nation who will not obey; not only their parents, but God as well because some youth of today are not in touch with reality in life. They seem to be in touch with self-identity: *The who am I* phase.

Teachers, Educators, and Parents Responsibility

They do not know who they are. Therefore they are constantly searching for ways to assimilate or affiliate themselves in society. God said, "He would raise up a nation that shall obey." I believe He will, but in the process, parents and teachers must try to help the children to make sound judgment and good decisions in life.

Teachers, Educators, and parents can make a difference in children lives by using good common sense and being persistent. One example is: rather than being physical abusive to a child when he misbehaves, maybe they should pray for the child in his/her presence. In the prayer, they should *rebuke* some of the *disobedient habits* that the child has. Teachers need to establish a unique rapport to find their niche with the children that they teach by meeting them halfway with their social problems, rather than letting the experts tell them how to discipline these students whom they are teaching.

Experts are good in verbal knowledge, but the teacher has to find a way to make their experiences work for them in the classroom. After I taught for many years, I learned that "experience is the best teacher." Teachers do learn how to captivate the student's behavior by using a variety of materials and activities geared to individuals, small groups, and large groups.

They must learn how to get every student involved in the learning process every day by using special techniques. The process of discipline is a big job.

You may have heard parents and other people talk about how terrible children are today. They have forgotten the reason for any child's behavior is because their parents are their children's first role model and first teacher; later comes the classroom teachers, pastors, coaches, other educators, church school teachers, and etc. These are the people who exemplify "good or bad behavior." These are the people who need to **THINK.!**

Parents' Thoughts!

*** Have we done all that we can do to help our children with their problems?

*** Have we used the day by day approach having a positive attitude, or are we always frustrated around our children or at them for some reason?

*** Do we model the right kind of Christian behavior that is necessary to instill good moral values in our children? And are we obedient to God in front of our children at all times? Children learn from what they see us do.

*** Do we speak the vernacular that is free of profanity, slang, or derogatory terms that we would not like to hear our children speak?

*** Are we selective about the kind of programs our children watch on TV daily? Do we understand the negative influence that TV has upon our children?

*** Why not take a holiday from TV for three to four days out of a month? This time may increase a child's ability to learn how to enjoy other things, such as: reading different types of literature that is just as meaningful as reading schoolbooks.

*** Do we keep good literature and materials to read on the coffee table or do we have "Playboy Magazines" lying around?

*** Do we realize that the major problem that our children are faced with in school today is "Do your own thing Generation?"

*** Do we listen to the music that the youth are playing on the radio? If so, what is it teaching them? -- Bad Behavior or Good Behavior?

*** If you are faced with any of the questions above, you must remember that much of the education that children have stem from their home environment. It is your duty and

Who is Responsible for the Child's Action?

responsibility to provide your children with a good home training and a good education.

Children must be taught by the parent to learn how to make good choices, or the right choice at home and teachers must reinforce those skills at school.

Parents must also remember that school is a minute part of their society and society has so much to offer children, some good and some bad. Talk with your child's teacher frequently to see how well he is doing in school.

Remember that parents of today have to deal with the issue of *things*. Parents have to build or purchase a new or big house because the Jones' have one. They have to drive the SUV because it is the going style automobile of today.

Their children must wear designers' clothing so that they will fit into the norms of name brand clothing or otherwise they will feel inferior about what they are wearing and will not want to go to school.

It is okay to have all of those things, but the parents must remember that they need to teach life's skills at home too, such as: Teach children how to assort clothes to be put into the washer, how to fold clothes after they have been dried, how to organize clothes to be put into the drawers, how to put clothes on the hangers to be put into the closets, put their shoes in the closet in the right place, put their dirty clothes into the hamper rather than throw them on the floor, put dishes in the dishwasher, put dishes in the cabinets after they have been washed, clean their room, makeup their bed in a neat manner, rake the leaves if they have trees, and take out the garbage. None of these chores are strenuous.

They must also complete all of their homework before they go to bed, if possible and put it in their book bag, so that the next morning it will not be left at home.

Parents need to read the Bible to the young children and teach the older children how to read the Bible themselves. They also need to keep good moralistic books available for the children to see and read them for enrichment daily.

Time is important too. Parents should turn the TV and radio off and have quiet time periodically. This should instill in the child how to be quiet in school and other places. Also it will train them how to become good listeners.

Children should be told and put to bed at a reasonable time so that they can get a good night's sleep. Also they must get up on time to take their shower, get dressed, comb their hair, brush their teeth, eat their breakfast, and get to the bus stop on time.

Before the child leaves home, he must be told to follow all school rules without faltering.

If those skills are instilled in a child at an early age, as he gets older, these characteristics will become natural. The child will also learn that there are consequences to every action. Consequences may be positive or negatives, they are based on you, the parent, and the way you give directions to your child for each chore.

The reason why parents should start at an early age with this training is that the younger the child the more his mind is developing and is opened for new knowledge. He will also develop an understanding of the way matters work.

The middle age child will not learn as quickly and easily as the younger child will if he misses these skills. Therefore the parent will have to give the middle age child an opportunity to make

Conflict at Home and at School

choices and hope that he will make the right ones. As I reflect back when I was in middle school, strangely as it may seem today, academics have not changed much, but conduct has. Many teachers cannot teach because of some students' conduct. In the past, the most the students would do was talk about your clothes or your MAMA! Now your "MAMA"! Was a fight! Every now and then a fistfight might break out among the boys, very rarely did the girls fight.

My belief is that our parents instilled in us that we were sent to school for a purpose, which was to get educated and that was their expectation. Secondly, our day at school always began with a ritual such as a Bible verse, the Lord's prayer, Psalms 23, or a lecture from our parents. All Moral standards were respected in school. If the students did not follow the rules of the school, corporal punishment was used at school and many times at home. Most students did not like corporal punishment; especially if they were going to get it twice.

Today students know that corporal punishment cannot be used without the parents' consent. Therefore, they are not afraid of the teachers or the administrators. They will tell the teacher quickly, you cannot punish me without my parents' consent. This type of behavior is exemplified because of the evils of the world have so much influence on our children that seems to be better than what the parents, teachers, or religious centers can. Children are faced with all kinds of crises. The middle grade child is under a lot of pressure from his peers. He may be influenced with drugs, alcohol, smoking cigarettes, and other drugs, gangs, sinful "Rap" music, robbing, stealing, abusive parents, teenage pregnancy, rape, and etc. Then the parents cannot understand why children act the way they do. Who should we blame – the child or the parent? Who should make the decision in the house? Who is in charge? Who is the authority figure in the home? The parents should be. Their children success depends on them.

It has been proven that children who are disciplined at home will discipline themselves at school and other places. They are well balanced. Most of them show good self-esteem, make good choices, are excellent leaders, have patience, show respect for their teachers and peers and do not use the school for a social outlet.

The younger children who do not have good training at home come to school upset with their parents or other people. Many times they will not have their homework completed, they may not have pencils or paper, books are usually left at home, and sometimes they interrupt the class every chance they get. They feel unhappy and unsuccessful because they cannot explain what is happening to them. They do not know how to avoid conflict. They feel threatened by their teachers and classmates. They seek refuge by tuning the teacher out. They turn a deaf ear to what the teacher is saying. They fear that they do not know the answer and the children will tease them or make smart comments. Those children usually have low self-esteem and will not talk about their problems. This is the time the teacher must show the student who is in charge. The teacher must sit down and talk to the child about his/her feelings alone. The one on one relationship might give the child a sense of worth. Hopefully by this time, the teacher will have learned how to master the 4 – "Ps" effectively. (Prayer at home, patience, persistence and perseverance).

The middle grade student does not deal with conflict in that manner. They have a different style.

They usually avoid conflict by hanging out with the tough guys or girls.

They refuse to acknowledge that there is conflict by pretending that it does not exist. They might quietly go along with others, or accept poor treatment while feeling angry or resentful. They might ignore their friend's inconsiderate acts but complain about it to their peers or other students later.

Generally the students will withhold their feelings: Avoid voicing their opinion or feelings so that they will not recognize their anger.

They will often accommodate troublemakers. They feel that it is better to agree than disagree or give in so that harm will not be brought upon them.

However those middle graders who are "confronters" will meet conflict "Head-On." Many times it will make sense, especially if the troublemaker is physically attacking them and there is not an adult around to protect them.

They must fight back to protect themselves. The confronter will never resolve a conflict, but they will defend themselves or their position. They will argue the point that they are right. Many times they will become very loud, boisterous, sarcastic, outspoken, threatening, verbally, or physical abusive. However, they still hide their feelings by not talking about themselves.

Finally, the Middle Grader is not necessarily a problem solver, but a compromiser. They will give something rather than get something. Sometimes they do communicate with others by sharing some of their feelings. And other times they began to collaborate with each other about other things. Collaboration takes a lot of effort and tedious undertaking because it requires talking and maybe being honest about their feelings. Most of the times, they do not like to share their feelings.

Parents, what should we do about the children who are dealing with these issues?

Have we created "robots" in our society? The only way children will respond to us is by pushing the right button? What force is strong enough to change our children way of thinking? Is it too late to use the *parenting philosophy*, which means to talk to your children? Or should we consult God to help us with dealing with them?

President George Bush – CNN Live, August 21, 2002, seems to think that "parents need to change their culture, be responsible for decisions made in life, love your children with all your heart and soul, and love your neighbor as you do yourself."

Many of us who are educators will agree with President Bush because this is one time teachers can become culturally biased without prejudice. Teachers can offer suggestions and encouragement to parents and students on ways to strengthen the child's behavior in academics and good conduct to a higher level of thinking and raise their standards. And also recommendations can be made on how to cope with these matters.

Listed below are sixteen steps toward "Better Discipline and Moral Values in the Classroom:

1.   Non Verbal and verbal communication between parents, teachers, and students are essential.

2.   All students must be challenged academically, socially, emotionally and morally daily.

3.   Social activities may increase or decrease a student's ability to communicate effectively.

4.   Multicultural education has become very prevalent in our society today. Basically because many countries believe in traditions, some of them believe that education is not important.

5.   Teachers must be free of racial prejudice and ethnic centrist if they are to be effective with their teaching of students from diverse backgrounds.

6.   Let students know that our society demands academic excellence.

7.   Have we ceased teaching about morals and values in the classroom? What is taking its place? Drugs, lottery, smoking, stealing, the pressure of terrorism, or the lack of the study of the Bible?

8.   Parent and teachers should remember that ethicality and identity play a major role in the student's life.

9.   Many teachers recognize that some students learn best when they are allowed to actively engage themselves in specific group projects and or activities.

10. Ethnicity and potential destitute both relate to individual differences and may cause cultural conflict among students.

11. Parents and teachers should be made aware that a student's self-perception affects his level of performance.

12. Parents and teachers should understand that stereotyping students is obsolete. Praise is more prevalent.

13. Parents and teachers should understand that images both positive and negative affect a child's behavior.

14. Teachers and parents remember that teaching discipline in school is a positive aspect and there are long-term solutions and consequences to every problem.

15. Parents and teachers should listen to the child and make suggestions or offer choices, rather than give orders or take action immediately.

16. Finally, parents and teachers should be able to determine what role religion plays in a child's life and build on those skills.

Working Word List

Today education has become one of the most important aspects in our society. Administrators and teachers have to start early planning each year to prepare for an excellent school year. They must develop new motivational strategies, new ideas, new methods of teaching those skills and objectives, and to promote the best possible standards to prevent problems in the future for our children. In order to do this they must develop a word list as a working guide to follow in their preparation. A few words are listed below.

Word List:

Purpose questions Answers Scientific-Space Age plan Ethics strategies comments complimentary competitive information-words rules directions optimistic pessimistic pragmatic contrast evaluation synthesize analyze similarities conclusion table conduct discipline statistics graph agreement positive disagreement pluralism desperation deprivation democracy chastisement capitalism Negative

Also we need to establish a *"Life Long"* skill list for teachers and students (Teacher's discretion based on experiences).

- ❖ **Apologize when wrong**
- ❖ **Think for yourself**
- ❖ **Be an independent learner**
- ❖ **Manipulation is not important**
- ❖ **Stay focused**
- ❖ **Plan ahead**
- ❖ **Lying is not necessary**
- ❖ **Involve students in decision making**

- ❖ Take responsibility for your own action
- ❖ Winning and losing are both significant characteristics
- ❖ Tolerant level is very important when frustration and anger arise
- ❖ Use a good sense of humor
- ❖ Be realistic
- ❖ Use good common sense
- ❖ America was built on a democracy
- ❖ Parents, students, and teachers should promote positive thinking in any given situation
- ❖ Patience and love changes hearts
- ❖ Peace stables the mind
- ❖ Every student should know that he is unique and special
- ❖ Remember the *Golden Rule*
- ❖ Find ways to deal with disappointment

Julia M. Hayes

Discipline the Whole Child

When we think of disciplining a child, we are faced with many unanswered questions. First we must look at the whole child. We cannot study just his attitude or personality, but every human organ in him. Perhaps starting with the DNA (deoxyribonucleic acid). We know that "when cells reproduce, they pass down offspring information on how to live, grow, and in turn reproduce. This information is carried on in the cell's nucleus. Each nucleus contains small parts called chromosomes... Every human cell contains 23 pairs of chromosomes" which are lined with genes.

But, as teachers, we cannot look at a child's DNA, but we can look at his personality and attitude to compare and contrast his behavior with that of his parents' and the approach that they use with the child's teacher. Teachers learn a lot about the child from just speaking with the parent. The teacher can pick up on how some of the child's mother's traits influence his behavior, and how his genetic make-up appears to be that of his father's. (Seeing is believing). Those are matters that should be considered when instructing a child. The teacher should try to look at the child as an individual throughout the teaching process.

Other concerns are: What is the child's living conditions like? Does he live with his father and mother, or are they separated or divorced? Who gets him ready for school each day? Has he had a good nutritious breakfast before he leaves home? Is he being treated fairly by his parents? Does he have siblings, if so, how many and how old are they? Is he faced with child neglect or child abuse? Does he complain about not feeling well? Does his parents love him? Does he attend church, church school, or any moral institution? Is he involved in sports or any kind of outside activities? What is behind those glarey eyes? How does he think? Does he have nervous ticks, does he speak in complete sentences? If the child is disruptive, should we continue to accept his bad behavior? Or what request should we initiate to reach this child to bring him into reality?

Julia M. Hayes

Real Account

A few years ago I had the opportunity to meet Sam (alias name). He was by far the most peculiar student I had encountered throughout my teaching career. This is a real account of my acquaintances with Sam in my class.

One August day a few years ago, I met Sam. Sam was usually the first child in my room each morning, or he was standing by my door when I arrived. Day one, I reminded him that he needed to wait in the cafeteria with the other students until the bell rang. Of course he did not like being in the cafeteria with the other students because he did not like crowds. As I opened the door, he would rush right in and sit in someone else's seat.

I learned later that this was the prompt to get my attention. I ignored him at first, hoping that he would finally get into his seat. I knew right off that I was going to undergo a problem, but I waited until I could grasp what was wrong with him before I started to chastise him.

I'M OK IF YOU'RE OK!

Each morning I decided to treat Sam with love, patience, respect, and all the kindness that I could give. It was hard!

48

Dialogue

Teacher: How are you doing this morning, Sam?

Sam: Fine! I had a great morning!

Teacher: That's good! What made your morning so great?

Sam: ...because I got up, fixed my breakfast, and I had the chance to do what I wanted to.

Teacher: My, you're smart! What time does your mother leave for work?

Sam: I don't know. Most of the time she's gone when I wake up.

I knew then that I had a problem. If he could do what he wanted to at home, it would be hard for him to cooperate with my students and me at school. And that is just what happened!

When I stopped talking to him and began to do my work, he would begin to stare at me and say, "Mrs. Hayes, I don't like you, I don't like what you're wearing today, I don't like your shoes, they look like old folks' shoes. And why can't we call you Mrs. H? (all in one breath).

I was stunned. I had been teaching two decades and no child had ever told me that he/she did not like me on the first day of school! I was flabbergasted! Most of my students loved me on the first day of school! I was embarrassed at first. Then I thought- this is going to be one of those year that I have heard teachers' talk about! And I am determined to remember the "4-Ps" and use them faithfully with this kid. Students were never rude to me on the first day or the first week of school. I did not respond to Sam at that moment. I had to keep my composure. Therefore, I kept my lips sealed tightly! Then I began to think and observe him. I knew I had to pray before I spoke to him again. I began to pray silently in the classroom. I had to know how to deal with this problem without embarrassing Sam or myself. I had to be a professional who would teach him how to walk in the light and not in the darkness. I had to change his way of thinking. I was faced with the dilemma of looking at this child every morning who had a real problem and he chose to take it out on me. For a while I just ignored him, no matter what he said to me, I just acted as if I did not hear him. Many times when you ignore a student who is out of order, he will stop. However, this was not the case. The more I ignored him, the worse he became. When Sam realized that he could not keep my attention, he started with the students in the room. He would bully them and made threats on them. Some of the students were afraid of him, therefore

The Conference Began

they would go along with him to keep him from intimidating them. When he made silly remarks, they would laugh with him. Daily, he would continue to get into someone's seat until I made him get out. He would call the students fat, ugly, liars, anything to antagonize them. He was very critical of everyone. I knew that I would not allow him to continue to create disturbances with the students or me any longer. The chastisement began. I started by analyzing and monitoring his behavior daily.

I kept him in the class one morning to talk to him about his conduct. He was angry with me because he would miss PE. He used several choice words. At this point it did not matter with me. I was ready to go to whatever direction I needed in order to correct his behavior.

Teacher: Sam, what is your problem?

Sam: Problem! I don't have a problem, you do!

Teacher: Tell me what you think is wrong with me.

Sam: I don't like you!

Teacher: And!

Sam: You don't teach us right! We don't understand that math! You teach us on a level too high! You need to "Rap" to us – We can learn it better. My old teacher use to do that.

Teacher: Well Sam, I am not a "Rapper." Do you have any suggestion on how I should "Rap" to you in Math?

Sam: No, but I know we can learn it better if you "Rap" to us. That's something we can understand.

Teacher: Sam, you are the only person who has spoken to me about not understanding Math. You have only been here for a short while, give it a few days and see if you can learn math my way. However, I will address the subject to see if any other students feel your way. If they do, I will give them the same assignment that I am going to assign to you. I want you to choose a math skill that you do not understand well and put it into a "Rap" song for me. If it has merit and is done well, I will let you teach it to the class one day and I will include it into my lesson plans. By Monday, let me know what you came up with. Well, that was the end of that. He never got anything together. He was on to something else.

Sam: You don't like us do you?

Sam: You are use to teaching those upper-ty kids and you think they are better than we are!

Teacher: Where did you get that idea from? I have never discussed any of the students whom I have taught in the past with you.

Then Sam began to tell me what his mother said about me.

I ignored that part of the discussion because I had never met his mother and she did not know me. This was about the third week in school and I knew I had to solve this problem. I told Sam that I was going to send a note home by him for his mother to attend a conference with me.

Sam: She ain't coming! She never comes to any conferences.

Teacher: What time does your mother get home today?

Sam: I don't know. Sometimes she gets home before I go to bed and other times she leaves before I get up in the morning. So I don't know when you can catch her! She likes her boyfriend! Most of the time she is with him. I don't like him!

Conference Time

I knew I had encountered another problem, the boyfriend. But I continued to talk to Sam because I knew he needed a friend. This was the one time I wanted to say to him, let me pray for you! But I could not say that. That was another example of deprivation of teaching and Freedom of speech! I did not have the choice to speak freely! Again, this was the time when I knew that our United States Constitution had failed us. Secondly they took the prayer out of the school and corporal punishment which left the teachers and administrators with no defense for disciplining children in the public schools.

Because I take my religion seriously, I did pray for Sam. However, he never knew it. I wanted to witness to him morally, but I could not. However, I knew Sam was acting-out of "Desperation and Deprivation!" He was lonely, he needed his parents to show affection toward him. He was put into an adult situation with cooking, ironing, washing his clothes, and getting ready for school and getting there the best way he could. I learned later that Sam should have been riding the bus, but he was missing it because of his chores and that was the only outlet that he had. Sam always tried to act so cool by hiding his emotions. He told me that he did not want anyone to feel sorry for him. He could always do it himself. He did not like me because I was the opposite of his mother. I cared for him and tried to get through to him that I did care. It took him for a while to began to trust me.

Julia M. Hayes

Conference with Mom! -- "Chaos!"

He didn't trust anybody at first but his old teacher. I was not able to talk to him about Jesus Christ, but I was able to continue to show him love, affection, and compassion, in spite of all of his misbehaving. I had to help turn his life around. One day we were talking about the things that he could do at home when he was alone. He told me that he did not complete his homework because he did not have anyone to help him. He could stay up as late as he wanted to. He could talk on the phone late at night. When I asked him who was he talking to, he said, some friends. I tried to get him to tell me who his friends were, but he would not.

Once I realized that Sam did not have anyone to help him with his homework, I stopped worrying about it. I decided to help him as much as I could at school until I could speak to his parents.

I finally got in touch with his Mom to set up a conference. That was the most chaotic situation I had ever encountered. When I put in the call to her, first of all, she was angry with me because I interrupted her work schedule. Secondly, she said, You must be in trouble! Why are you calling me? I explained to her that I was not in trouble, but her son was.

He was in danger of failing academically, and his conduct was awful. And I needed her or his father to come in for a conference so that we could set up an academic and conduct plan to help get her son through the school year without failing.

I told her that Sam was a bright child and all he needed was to be steered in the right direction. After a long drawn out conversation with her, bashing me every chance she could get, she finally gave in when she realized that I was not going to give in without a conference then she agreed to come in.

Sam's Mom got there late, angry because she had to get off her job and would not be paid for that time. She looked very untidy. Her hair was not combed, she was dressed shabby, wore bedroom shoes, and definitely no make-up.

I said Good morning, and that did it. She said I did not like her son and we had a "personality conflict!" I was not telling the truth about Sam not having his homework because she "called home daily, and he told her that he had finished it. The next morning she asked him before she left for work and he said that he did it. And her child did not lie! She said that I was one of those *Big Shot* teachers who did not understand black children, especially her son. She could tell by the way I talked! She did not want me to put any pressure on him to be a role model for other kids because he was his own role model. She just wanted me to give him his assignments and he would do them.

I waited until she finished, then I asked her if she was aware that I had sent home four missing work forms. She said no. She said that Sam never showed them to her. Then she got angry with Sam. She told me to bring Sam in there. I did. Sam came in with tears in his eyes. He knew he was in trouble. However, he stood up for himself. When she asked him about the missing assignments, he told her that she was never there to receive them – She was never home when he was awake. He said, "Most of the time I am asleep when you get home at night and asleep when you leave in the morning. How can I give them to you to sign? I have to do everything for myself. I don't like being alone that is the reason why I act like I do". I told Sam's Mom I could understand now why he has not done his homework, but why doesn't he do his class work in school? I wanted to know if she knew that he was not doing any schoolwork at all. She said that she never asked him about schoolwork because she wanted him to be responsible enough to do his work without her help. She expressed that he was old enough to do it without her. She

Julia M. Hayes

said that she had not had any trouble with him getting his work before – and his teachers liked him. Then she flew in a rage with Sam. I let them battle it out-back and forth. When they calmed down, I went back to the same question. What are we going to do about Sam? Are we going to let him fail? I invited you here today to set up a plan to help Sam get on the right track of learning to his fullest potential. I told her we needed to develop two plans: An Academic Plan and a Conduct Plan.

She granted me the permission to set up an Academic Plan, but Sam should be allowed to speak freely and express himself. She did not want to curve his expression. She said, "Everybody needs to talk at some times." We did not allow the students to talk at school ever. She thought that I was too strict on Sam. I needed to give him more freedom. She did not know what kind of teacher I was!

Sam's Mom did the typical thing that most parents do when they do not discipline their children. They blame the teacher for his failures.

I continued to listen to her and take notes. The 3rd time and the last time I told her what her reason was for being there. I said to her, your child is at the point of FAILING in both: Academics and Conduct. If nothing is done within the next two weeks he will fail based on what he has already done. I want us to help him. I do hope you are aware that your child's conduct can and has affected his inability to learn academically. It has also affected other children's learning. She finally agreed to let us set up a plan for academics but she would not be able to follow through with me because she was the "Bread Winner" and she would not be able to check his work on a daily basis, neither could she help him with home work. So we set up the plan for her to assist him on the weekend if she had time. I also reminded her that it would be her responsibility to see to it that Sam showed her his school work and homework.

56

My Point of View

Sam's mother worked with Sam and me for a while. But she never apologized to me, neither did she agree that she needed to help Sam with his work. And she made no plans to correct his behavior in school. Later on, I learned that she had some problems. So I turned the matter over to the counselor and social worker.

I did not want to be one of those teachers who became prejudice unwaveringly. Prejudice to me is an erroneous judgment, usually with negative ideas, which is based on faulty information. Also prejudice can lead into stereotyping and labeling children. Therefore, I would not allow myself to get into thinking on that level. My expectation of Sam was not going to be a myth or assumption that his behavior in conduct exemplified his home training alone. After all, he was a preadolescent and that accounted for some of his faulty actions.

As an educator, I had to differentiate between "Bad Behavior" and desperation for attention. Considering the number of years teaching using school rules as a base in the classroom, I should have been more prepared for this type of behavior. But because we are human, our expectations vary. Many times we are not prepared for such action. Sam's behavior was different from any other child's that I had taught. He was belligerent, insulting, threatening, bullying, and sarcastic to the students and me. He had no respectable person to insult. His behavior lead to misunderstanding and conflict between us. I realized that we must come to some kind of mutual agreement if I was going to continue to teach him without showing partial judgment throughout the year. Two of my best characteristics are: "prayer and patience."

Julia M. Hayes

"A Voice in The Past"

Over the years, I often refer back to Dr. Benjamin E. Mays' "a voice in the past" quotes on education. He said, "You are what you aspire to be, and not what you now are; you are what you do with your mind, and you are what you do with your youth." He goes on to talk about how he is disturbed and uneasy about man because we have no guarantee that when we train a man's mind, we will train his heart; there is no guarantee that when we increase a man's knowledge, we will increase his goodness. And finally he says, There is no necessary correlation between knowledge and goodness.

Sam was a perfect example of this. He had knowledge but did not know how to exemplify or show goodness. No matter how much I tried to train him to behave in a respectable manner so that he could concentrate on his lesson and get along with his peers, seemingly, there was something inside of him "saying, don't follow those directions – just continue to do what you have been doing! -- You're Okay!"

Sam's behavior was a wake-up call for me. I knew I had to go beyond the call of duty to solve this problem. So I did.

Sam's schoolwork was never as good as it could have been if his mother had been consistent. Sam and I continued to have conferences throughout the year. I put Sam on an academic contract, which gave him the freedom to work at his own pace at school. And I put him on a behavior checklist for conduct. He enjoyed working with the contract because he did not like people. I told Sam that he had special habits that he had chosen to handle differently from other children. They were "anger and fear." I explained to him how he could change those habits of negatives into positives. I repeatedly talked to Sam about his behavior. I took anecdote notes on him weekly as we had our conferences. The conference brought about a change in his life. He was able to see and

58

acknowledge his mistakes. We talked about choices. Did he make good choices or bad ones during the week. He had the options to join the class and work harmoniously as long as he obeyed and followed the classroom rules. I reminded Sam that hopefully he had learned that it was not okay for him to insult his peers or teachers. Yes, I knew he had feelings, and it was OK to feel, even if they were bad. It was OK if he expressed his feelings, but in the right manner. Also it was time for him to accept responsibility for his own actions. I said to him that his mother loved him and she wanted him to do well in school. But time and patience had not let her help him in the way that she wanted to. I talked to him about having Faith in me as his teacher and a person who really were concerned about his welfare. I knew he had some good in him so I never let the bad part of him overpower the good.

Julia M. Hayes

Solution to Problems

My goal was to win the battle. Did I win? I think I did. Sam finally admitted that I really cared about how children learned and I did help him to get on the right road. Near the end of school, Sam began to blend in with the other students in the room. For me, that was a perfect blend of my use of the 4 P's along with consistency and firmness. I could not let Sam be another statistic on the streets. This was one of my most challenging years of teaching. I suffered through it, I over came the desperation of helping Sam learn. I encountered a few other Sams during my years of teaching, but I was OK as long as I won the battle!

In my opinion, the Middle Grade students seem to have more trouble than any other children do in school. Perhaps because they are going through a series of changes in their lives. Their bodies are changing physically, mentally, and emotionally. These are normal steps for the pre-adolescence. One should not compare or contrast siblings' behavior, looks, attitudes, or personalities because they are individuals. Many adults make the mistake of making comparisons. One suggestion for parents and teachers is to let the child know that mistakes are going to be made. And they must put in time to understand the child, themselves, and the situation. They should implement family time and class time for discussing matters that might affect their children. Parents and teachers should become good listeners too. Parents and teachers should set up goals and objectives at home and at school to prevent hassles and problems in the future.

Many times when teachers have more than one child misbehaving in the classroom, it is time for a "Roundtable Discussion." They must remember to always have the "What" and "How" list of questions prepared before trouble arises. Parents must use such motivational factors as: the 4- Ps (prayer, patience, persistence and perseverance) and also

60

remind their children that they have faith in them that they will do the right thing in life. They must express that sometimes when things do not go well, or they might not get what they expect. Maybe they should rethink of their goals and realize that failing is not so bad as long as one can recuperate from it and reach for higher levels. Those words should instill in the child to have courage, faith, and respect. Also, children should be taught that they are individuals and they will be loved, trusted, and respected as individuals. Children must be made aware that life brings disappointments and they should be

Survey II

able to adjust to them as they work through them. Sometimes children will feel alienated or depressed, maybe at this time, just a hug will cure the solution to the problem. *Why not be Blessed and not Stressed*?

When ever your child has a discipline problem at school, be opened for a general discussion. Listen to your child's point of view. Find out if he realized that he had other alternatives. Ask him if he could have made better choices, or did he think that his behavior was appropriate for solving the problem.

A survey was taken using randomly selected subjects; ages 19 years to 60 years and older. These were college students, parents or grandparents of children ages 1 year – 19 years. Their occupations varied from managerial, teachers, project managers, data entry, tech, church director of Protective Services, store clerks, program managers, multi-media administrators, professional educators, day care directors, ministers of the gospel, counselors, paralegals, administrators in the public schools, housewives, and home-school Moms.

Each subject was given the same survey. The survey consisted of eight questions. Each question dealt with problems that related to "Bad Behavior," religion, and the use of moral standards at home and at school.

Hypothesis

My hypothesis stated that there was a minimum relationship in the way parents and teachers dealt with children with "Bad Behavior" and "religion" played a minor role in disciplining children at home and at school.

As you view the lists and Bars later, you will observe that research showed that one of the major problem that children are faced with today is the breakdown of the family structure. It is a major issue. It was rated number one on the List. Peer Pressure was rated number two, especially with the middle age child, and drugs were rated number three. I was surprised to see that sex and violence were rated so closely. They were only one half point apart, with sex rating 4.5 on the scale while violence rated 4 points. According to the subjects, they believe that Economic Environment and the Political System rarely affected a child's behavior at home, school, and in society.

Statistics

The study indicated furthermore that a child should be responsible for his own behavior at school and the parents should be secondary in this matter.

I strongly disagree with this finding because I believe that a parent is ultimately responsible for his children's performance, no matter where they are. They make the difference. They should prepare the child for school each day before he leaves home. A parent's rules determine how well the child behaves in school. I cannot express enough the parents' position in disciplining their children. They are their first role model, and their first teacher. They establish ethics and values, which deal with morality, emotional aspects, social settings, and raising the standards. Parents have the authority to raise the Bar or lower it, depending on their decision and choices that they make for their children.

Statistically, according to the survey, it showed that the Bar elevated when the question was asked: Should *religion* play a part in the child's life at all times?

The Bar was raised extremely high. 70% said **YES**. 18% said **NO**. And 12% were undecided.

Also when the question was asked: Should *religion* play a role in disciplining children? The Bar was raised again extremely high. 65% thought it should, 20% thought that it should not, and 15% were undecided.

One subject said that "*religion* can be a sound foundation in the rearing and discipline of a child. *Religious* teaching aids parents in teaching their children values, morals, and other life's skills that cannot or is not permitted to be taught anywhere but at home or church."

Another kindergarten teacher conveyed that, "Reading the Bible helps us to discipline children in the correct way. It helps us to discipline with love, and care for our children."

Finally, an educator stated that "*religion* should play a major role in a child's life because the belief and study of God is a life changing experience. It constitutes faith, hope, love, and peace which is completely opposite of what the world offers."

When subjects were asked if *religious* concepts such as: Lord, God, Jesus Christ, and prayer be used as a strategy to help improve students' attitudes, personalities, or "Bad Behavior" at home and at school, the Bar was lowered.

45% said no, 35% said yes, and 20% said it did not matter. However, one subject said that "these concepts must first begin at home. No one should teach about Jesus if he/she does not know him personally." And on the other hand, another subject believes that "Rather than concepts, I feel that a relationship with the Lord, Jesus Christ should be fostered in children in order to improve their behavior, attitudes, and etc."

A parent who is a Program Manager, suggested that: "To understand these concepts, is to understand the fear and reverence that are due. I personally would prefer that my children give a higher regard to the ramifications relative to our religious knowledge than the congruencies relative to me at the point the two may be able to be separated. Religion that is true, negotiates change in our attitudes, personalities and *bad behavior* any and everywhere." These concepts should be used only if a parent gives consent because there are so many different religions in the school."

Final question: Should religious concepts such as: Psalms 23, The Ten Commandments, or the Lord's Prayer be taught in the public schools as a form of discipline? Again, the Bar was lowered.

45% said **NO**, 25% said **YES**, and 30% said it did not matter.

Survey – II Results:

Question # 1:   What problems do you feel that pre-adolescents and adolescents are facing today?   Number in order of importance – one being the highest priority.

Age Group: Range – 19 years – 60 and over.

1.   Break down of the family structure
2.   Peer Pressure
3.   Drugs
4.   Sex
5.   Violence
6.   Smoking
7.   Diseases
8.   Economic Environment
9.   Media Influences
10.   Political System
11.   Technology
12.   Suicide

Question # 2: Should religion play a major role or minor role in a child's life? Explain your answer.

Age Group Range: 19 years -- 60 and over.

Figure # 1: Bar raised:

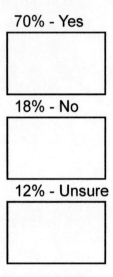

70% - Yes

18% - No

12% - Unsure

The Bar was raised extremely high. Most subjects said that religion should play a major role. 6% questioned whether religion meant Christianity or not. And 6% said that parents must decide for themselves. And if they raise their children in a loving structured home, there will be no doubt that the child will be successful.

Question # 3: Should religion play a major or minor role in the educational process of a child's life?

Age Group Range: 19 years – 60 and over

There was NO variation in the bars. The feelings were mutual.

Figure # 2

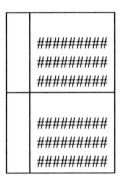

The survey showed that all subjects felt the same. They all thought that religion must be used in some way, but there were no agreement on how.

Question # 4: Should religion such as Christianity play a role in disciplining children?

Age Group Range: 19 years – 60 and over

The Bar was raised tremendously!

Figure # 3

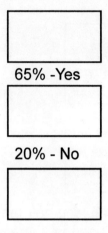

65% -Yes

20% - No

15% Undecided

With this high rating, I think that parents want their children to be raised in a Christian environment without biases, but do not know how to articulate this message to them for special purposes, such as: in school, at home, and in society.

Question # 5: Should religious concepts such as: Lord God, Jesus Christ, and prayer be used as a strategy to help improve students' attitudes, personalities or "Bad Behavior" in school?

Figure # 4   The Bar was lowered.

45% - No

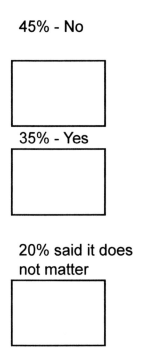

35% - Yes

20% said it does not matter

I think some parents would like to use religions such as the terms above, but they are afraid that they will be ridiculed about using them to speak-out on this issue.

Survey – II Results:

Subjects Age Range: 19 years – 60 and over

Question # 6: Who should be responsible for children's conduct in school? Number in order of importance with one being the greatest priority.

1.   Child

2.   Parents

3.   Teacher

4.   Assist. Principal

5.   Counselor

6.   Pastor

7.   Social Worker

8.   Psychologist

The majority of the raters thought that the child should be responsible for his conduct in school.

I firmly disagree. I can say this with reservation. Parents should be responsible for their children behavior, whether bad or good; in any given situation. I know this from experiences.

My hypothesis was right on target. Very rarely does this happen.

Survey Results: Figure # 5

Question # 7: Do you believe that religious concepts of any kind should be taught in public schools?

The Bar was lowered.

35.7% said Yes

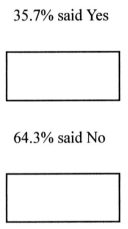

64.3% said No

This question seemed a little ambiguous to me at first. But when the subjects came to their conclusion, they saw it as having a clear-cut answer. No one was undecided.

I was not surprised at the results because we have so many different beliefs. Therefore it was hard to come to any one conclusion unless we all believe in the same almighty God. What do you think?

Hypothesis'   Conclusion:

My hypothesis stated that the results would show that there would be a minimum relationship in the way parents and teachers dealt with children with bad behavior and religion would play a minor role in disciplining children at home and in school.

My hypothesis was right on target. Very rarely does this happen.

The Bible Gives Parents the Authority to discipline their Children

God has left a set of guidelines for us to follow as we discipline our children and ourselves.

We, as adults must read the Bible to learn the ethics that God has provided for us. The Bible tell us to "train up a child in the way he should go and when he gets older he will not depart from it." Proverbs 22:6

Exodus 21:12 tells a child to Honor thy father and thy mother; that thy days may be long upon the land which the Lord thy God giveth thee.

Ephesians 6:1-4 tell children to obey their parents in the Lord: For this is right. Honour thy father and mother; which is the first commandment with promise; that it may be well with thee, and thou mayest live long on the earth. And, ye fathers, provoke not your children to wrath: but bring them up in the nurture and admonition of the Lord.

And parents should submit themselves to one another in fear of God. Eph. 5:21.

I strongly believe that God has a purpose and a plan for our lives and the more effective God's Plan is the more responsible and unconfined parents, teachers, educators, and other adults should become to talk to their children.

A child must be obedient to his parents. The Bible says, "Spare the Rod, or Spoil the Child." Many parents do not use the "rod" for fear of the laws of today. Some scholars seem to believe that *sparing the rod* does not mean hitting or forcing a child to do something, but steering him in the right direction.

At times I agree with them and other times I do not because it depends on the situation and the age of the child.

We have to be very careful today when disciplining children, especially if they are rebellious. Those children pick up on the law very quickly because they are looking for a way not to follow their parents' rules.

Obedience must be taught in order for the child to learn how to cope with everyday life and with their peers, parents, teachers, other family members, and people in general. They must learn how to cooperate, be respectful, be responsible, and have positive self-esteem.

All children should be told that even parents have to obey rules in society. They have to obey their bosses at work, their pastors at church, and most of all, they must obey God! Because God said, "If you love me, keep my commandments. Ex. 19:1-20... When we keep His commandments, we are being obedient to Him.

Today some middle age children view discipline as being a form of "Reward or Punishment." They seek rewards for doing things that are natural. If parents do not give them tangible items or money to complete a task, most of the time it will not get done. For those parents who use Reward and Punishment, I believe that this is a way of saying to your child that you only do right when I am around and have paid you to do so. That is not the right way! We do not want to teach that behavior to our children. We want to teach them to always be fair and honest. Do the right thing at all times. Follow your parents' rules. Show them that you can be responsible and respectful without them being there. This should build faith and trust between the parent and child.

Parents and Educators "Speak Out" On *Religious* Issues

"I believe that religion should be the child's way of life. The things they do and say should reflex their religion. So, I believe that religion should be the major role in a child's life.

Rena Swearingen, Stone Mountain, GA

"Yes, religion must be included to make man whole. We are spirits, souls, not just body."

L. Dillard, Teacher

"Students come from many religious backgrounds. The school should not teach religion because we live in a very religious and diverse culture."

R. Allen, Teacher

"Ethics and values should be taught at school. Religion might need to be an important part of some children's education – many roads to take."

J. Alvards, Norcross, GA

"Major – It has been proven that children who are surrounded by prayer do better later in life. A good foundation goes a long way."

Fannie Mitchell, Decatur, GA

"The way the world is today, Technology is the key. Without it, you will have no life. You will not be able to function in society."

Sherry Dennis, Lithonia, GA

"Yes, All students need to have the knowledge of God and his reality. Doing so, gives opportunity to the Holy Spirit to dwell and minister. I do not know that I would say that the concept of Christianity be taught exclusively in the public school system, but as the concept itself is very personal. But the knowledge of God promotes hope and faith develop at God's hand."

A. J. Jordan, Stone Mountain, GA

"I do not see religion as a part of academic education. There are academic skills and religious concepts. They are not the same."

D. T. H.

"Religion is one's own interpretation and knowledge of a higher being, whether learned or spiritually connected."

R. Allen, Teacher

"Once the foundation is built in a Christian environment, then it should not be taught in school. Public schools are to educate students for future careers. In the King James Version of the Holy Bible, Proverbs 22:6 says, Train up a child in the way he should go; and when he is old, he will not depart from it."

Jerlene Usher, Retired Data Entry

"I believe that Christian values and character building traits should be taught to children as part of the educational process. This would help to promote Christian love and respect for all of God's creation."

Charles Jones, Project Manager

"I think Christian principles should be taught in the public schools in America since this country was founded on Christian Principles. It's ironic that "IN God We Trust" is printed on our money, but is considered wrong to articulate that in the public schools.

Larnell Wilson, Stone Mountain

"I believe that religion is a lifestyle that should be lived daily. I know this because as a child I attended a Catholic School and was taught about God and Jesus; but until I started to live the lifestyle, I did not know of this type of peace and joy. Everyone can have this if they know God and live the lifestyle."

Selina Johnson, Teacher

"Education is wonderful. Children must learn about economics, language arts, math, history, and etc. But also, children must learn respect, friendship, love, compassion and peace, and this is best taught and lived through the spirit of God and the example we have is that of Jesus Christ.

Angelia Hayes, Educator

"with reservations – religion in the school somewhat creates a peaceful atmosphere for the student. It also reminds the child what he or she has been taught at home and in church. Also, the expectation demands respect while the child is away from those places. Therefore, we must remember that the rule that religion exercises, must be a part of the child's foundation at home and in agreement at school by both: parent and child."

Anonymous

Parents' TEST

Now that you have read about people's point of view on *religious* issues, conduct at home and at school, and parents' responsibility. What do you think? What is your feeling?

If you can answer 14 out of the 18 questions below correctly, you are on the right road to becoming a great parent. Be honest!

1. Do you make sure that your child eats a full RDA meal daily? (This does not include Fast Foods). Yes ___ No ___

2. Do you spend at least 16 hours each day with your child/children? Yes ___ No ___

3. Do you help your child with homework if needed? Yes ___ No ___

4. Do you assign chores to your child daily? Yes ___ No ___

5. Do you check to see if chores are completed before bedtime? Yes ___ No ___

6. Do you check your child's homework to see if it is completed before bedtime and have him put it in his book bag for the next day. Yes ___ No ___

7. Do you have a conversation time with your child/ children about their day during supper or before bedtime? Yes ___ No ___

8. Do you consult with your child's teacher periodically to keep up with how well he is doing in school? Yes ___ No ___

9. Do you read good literature to your child once or twice a week? Yes ___ No ___

10. Do you teach your child Christian and moral values such as prayer, respect and love? Yes ___ No ___

11. Do you listen to your child express his feelings about certain issues such as: Likes and Dislikes? Yes ___ No ___

12. Do you ever tell your child that many times we make mistakes? Yes ___ No ___

13. Does your child attend any moral institution such as Church, Church School, Bible Class, or a Christian School? Yes ___ No ___

14. Do you discipline your child when he does something wrong? Yes ___ No ___

15. Are you more inclined to use corporal punishment rather than explain to your child what he has done is wrong? Yes ___ No ___

16. Do you give your child a hug or a kiss daily? Yes ___ No ___

17. Do you tell your child that you love him/her periodically? Yes ___ No ___

18. Do you know and understand your child well? Yes ___ No ___

Could you answer all of the questions with a "Yes?" ___ If so, you passed the test. If No, What are you going to do to improve your status as a parent?

Julia M. Hayes

Conduct

Conduct is how you respond to things
Whether good or bad.
Conduct is how you feel
Whether happy or sad.

Conduct is where you go
To do right or wrong.
Conduct is how you express yourself
If you're singing in a song.

Conduct is how you define yourself
Whether intelligent or a little slow.
Conduct is how you finish questions
With either yes or no.

Conduct is how you speak to others
Whether nicely or mean.
Conduct is how you're treated
Even if you're as tiny as a bean.

Conduct is the way you show respect
Whether to an adult or to another peer.
Conduct is the way you listen
Or if you play like you can't hear.

Always remember conduct is you,
Your action and ways
Conduct is your brain and how you use it
Whether if you're as bright as the sun's rays!

By: James Knowles, III

Conduct is a matter of choices to chose
right or wrong
to be weak or strong.
Conduct is your behavior towards
other people
respectful or ungrateful
Somewhere along the road you make choices of
how you act
and decides if it is right or wrong.
but whatever you do hold your
head up
and
stand strong.
Life isn't always going to be fair because
of people's attitudes
Just carry yourself the right way and shoot for
long...latitudes.
Conduct is really about being yourself because
no one in this world is going to be you!

By: Jasmine Knowles

Acknowledgments:

This book is based on my life's journey as a teacher. I am grateful to those who helped to guide my efforts in expressing my feelings about education, "Bad Behavior" and Christian Beliefs in the public schools. I also want to commend those who took time out to complete surveys and expressed their honest opinion about the questions that were asked. I could not have written this book without the love and support of the people listed below and whom I consulted with periodically as my family, friends, colleagues, politicians, writers, Theologians, and church members:

My parents, Tommie L. Glover and my late father, Reverend Theodore Glover, who reminded me several times that I would become a teacher of education in the future.

Tannish H. Knowles, Angelia Hayes, and Virgil L. Hayes, who encouraged me to continue the struggle of promoting my education and forced me to grow far beyond my potential; and my grandchildren, James and Jasmine Knowles, whose poems are a part of this book and are my greatest fans.

I am grateful for friends who had faith in me and kept me going and believing through challenges large and small, that a change will come and those who completed the Survey Consent Form: Larnell Wilson, Rusha Lindsey, Selina Johnson, Jerlene Usher, Charles Jones, Auturo Jordan, Fannie Mitchell, Sherry Dennis, Denette Gardner, and Rena Swearingen.

Many thanks to Kathryn Jefferson, my prayer intercessor who interceded for me consistently for many years.

Special regards to Angelia Hayes, my daughter, a theology major of Emory University, Atlanta, Georgia, who has served as the camp's counselor for the last four years during summer camp.

I am appreciative to my colleagues who completed the survey and worked with me during the many struggling times while teaching in the public schools: Ernestine Johnson, Barbara Troup, Bernice Fuller, D.H.T. Jenny Alvarado, Larry Dillard, R. Allen, Pearl Gadson, Connie Wheeler and Cynthia McGuire Smith.

Many thanks to my pastor, Bishop James H. Morton, whom I have relied upon for Christian guidance for nineteen years.

I applaud the critics' notes that I have gathered from books, Television, newspapers, magazines, and etc. to help me get my point over to the readers. Special thanks goes to the President of the United States, George Bush, Washington, D.C., John B. Cobb, Professor of Claremont School of Theology, Claremont, CA, Marva Collins, author of *Ordinary Children, Extraordinary Teachers*, Norfolk, VA, Bishop Paul S. Morton, The Presiding Bishop of the Full Gospel Fellowship International Conference, New Orleans, LA, and many others whose books I have read and enjoyed.

With gratitude, I appreciate the authors of the following books: *The Night Swimmers*, by Betsy Byars, *Government by the People*, by James McGregor Burns, *The Holy Bible*, by Joseph Howard Gray, *Haunting Tales*, by Nathaniel Hawthorne, *Scholastic Book Club*, by Genes and Inheritance, *Where Do We Go From Here: Chaos or Community?* By Dr. Martin Luther King, Jr., *"A Voice in The Past"*, by: Dr. Benjamin E. Mayes, *Daily Bouquets*, by Helen Steiner Rice, and *A Book about God*, by Lee & Shepherd Company.

With gratitude and appreciation to my daughter, Tannish H. Knowles, for helping me to redesign the Survey Consent Form and proof reading the manuscript several times before it was published.

I love each one of you and in return, I hope that I can live up to the standards that you have set for me as an educator and friend.

Conclusion

Finally, I am responsible for all of the facts and opinions in this book. It gives me great pleasure in knowing that education is a major concept in our society, which is filled with issues such as: *problems in conduct* and *Bad Behavior* in school daily. Teachers still need help with that issue. My question still remains: Why cannot teachers use religion such as *prayer* as a discipline tool, to promote good conduct in the public schools? If parents, teachers and educators are consistent with it, I believe it will work! It never failed for me.

You be the judge. What Do You Think?

Bibliography

1. Byars, Betsy. *The Night Swimmers*. Illustrated by Troy Howell. Boston, MA: Houghton Mifflin Company, 1989.

2. President Bush, George. *"Parents Need to Change Their Culture.* CNN Live Television. Washington, DC: August 21, 2002.

3. James McGregor Burns and J.W. Pelteason. *Government by the People*. New Jersey: 8th Edition Prentice-Hall, Inc. Englewood Cliffs, New Jersey: 1952-1972.

Reynolds V. United States, (1879)

United States Constitution, First Amendment p. 99

Engel V. VITALE (1963)

Albington School District V. Schempp p. 101

Gitlow V. New York, p. 99

Cobb, John B. Jr. Professor of Theology Emertis, *"Religion and Education."* Claremont School of Theology, Claremont, California. 2002.

Collins, Marva. *Ordinary Children, Extraordinary Teachers*. Hampton Roads Publishing Company, Inc. Norfolk, VA: 1992.

"Genes and Inheritance." Scholastic Book Club. New York, NY: 2001

Gray, Joseph Howard, D.D. *Holy Bible*. Gethsemane Edition. Copyright, 1946 & 1948.
Proverb 22:6
Exodus 21:12
Ephesians 6:1-4
Ephesians 5:21
Exodus 19:1-20

Hayes, Angelia. *Church Connection Magazine*, (Georgia's Link to the Church Community). "Changing a Generation." Decatur, GA: 1995.

Hawthorne, Nathaniel. *Haunting Tales*. Dr. Heidegger's Experiment. Scholastic, Inc.

King, Martin Luther, Jr. Dr. *Where Do We Go From Here: Chaos or Community?* Boston, MA: Beacon Press, 1967.

Knowles, James W. Poem: *"Conduct."* Lakeside High School, Atlanta, GA: 2003.

Knowles, Jasmine M. Poem: *"Conduct."* Henderson Middle School. Chamblee, GA: 2003.

Mayes, Benjamin E. Dr. *"A Voice in the Past."* Morehouse College. Atlanta, GA: 1960's.

Morton, James H. Bishop. *"Parents are Ultimately Responsible for their Children's Behavior."* New Beginning Full Gospel Baptist Church Summer Camp. *Decatur, GA: 2000-2003.*

Morton, Paul S. Presiding Bishop of The Full Gospel Baptist Church Fellowship International Conference. : *"Changing A Generation by the Sword of the Spirit." (Georgia's Link to the Church Community). New Orleans, LA: 1996.*

National Research Survey. *"Christian Civic and Political Involvement"*. Hagerstown, MD: 2003.

Rice, Helen Steiner Foundation. *"Faith to Believe."* Copyright 1990 by Virginia J. Ruehlmann. Ravell Baker Book House Company. Grand Rapids, MI. 1990.

Saul, First King of Israel. *Children's Bible*. Paradise Press, 1998.

Weisgard, Leonard. Illustrator. *A Book About God*. Lothrop, Lee & Shepard Co., New York: 1953.

About The Author

Julia M. Hayes, a Christian educator for the past thirty-two years in the Georgia public school system has communicated with thousands of people collectively, along with her family and friends. Yet, few of them had heard of a first-hand - account of her extraordinary life as a master teacher in math and science, until her retirement program. Her goals and strategies included becoming a successful teacher and seed planter for all students. As a business owner of a tutorial academic program, she served as an administrator to help bridge the gap between homework and schoolwork. With much prayer, patience, persistence, and perseverance, she became an expert in positive disciplining and academics. She is the mother of two daughters and the grandmother of two.

Printed in the United States
25341LVS00005BA/1-102

9 781418 425371